GOOGLE CLASSROOM:

Google Classroom User Manual To Master Virtual Teaching. 2020 Useful Guide To Benefit From Distance Learning In Our Digital Era.

LARRY OXFORD

LARRY OXFORD

© Copyright 2020 - All rights reserved.

The content contained within this book may not be reproduced, duplicated or transmitted without direct written permission from the author or the publisher. Under no circumstances will any blame or legal responsibility be held against the publisher, or author, for any damages, reparation, or monetary loss due to the information contained within this book. Either directly or indirectly.

Legal Notice: This book is copyright protected. This book is only for personal use. You cannot amend, distribute, sell, use, quote or paraphrase any part, or the content within this book, without the consent of the author or publisher.

Disclaimer Notice: Please note the information contained within this document is for educational and entertainment purposes only. All effort has been executed to present accurate, up to date, and reliable, complete information. No warranties of any kind are declared or implied. Readers acknowledge that the author is not engaging in the rendering of legal, financial, medical or professional advice. The content within this book has been derived from various sources. Please consult a licensed professional before attempting any techniques outlined in this book.

By reading this document, the reader agrees that under no circumstances is the author responsible for any losses, direct or indirect, which are incurred as a result of the use of information contained within this document, including, but not limited to, — errors, omissions, or inaccuracies.

TABLE OF CONTENTS

INTRODUCTION 8

CHAPTER 1: THE BENEFITS OF GOOGLE CLASSROOMS 12

- EXPOSES BOTH TEACHERS AND STUDENTS TO ONLINE LEARNING 12
- SUPER EASY TO GET MATERIALS 12
- ALL WORK IS THERE 12
- CREATES COLLABORATIVE LEARNING 13
- STUDENTS TAKE OWNERSHIP 14
- OPENNESS 14
- PAPERLESS 15
- LIFEHACK 15
- DIFFERENTIATION 15
- CRITICISM 15
- INFORMATION ANALYSIS 16

CHAPTER 2: HOW TO START A PLAN BOOK FOR YOUR CLASS 18

- CREATE A LESSON 18
- GOOGLE FORMS 21
- USING CLASSWORK 23

CHAPTER 3: HOW TO CREATE A CLASS AND ORGANIZE IT 28

- STEP BY STEP INSTRUCTIONS TO CREATE A CLASS 28
- CUSTOMIZE THE APPEARANCE OF YOUR CLASS 28
- STEP BY STEP INSTRUCTIONS TO ADD STUDENTS TO GOOGLE CLASSROOM 29
- HOMEROOM COMMUNICATION 30
- ORGANIZING CLASS TOPICS 30
- ANNOUNCEMENTS 33

CHAPTER 4: HOW YOU CAN MANAGE THE DUE DATES, HOMEWORK, AND ASSIGNMENTS 36

- ORGANIZING STUDENTS PROJECTS 36
- HOW STUDENTS ACCESS ASSIGNMENTS 41
- TIPS ON CREATING DIFFERENTIATED ASSIGNMENTS ON GOOGLE CLASSROOM 42
- TIPS FOR MANAGING DIFFERENTIATED ASSIGNMENTS IN GOOGLE CLASSROOM 44
- STUDENT SUBMISSION OF ASSIGNMENTS 45

Scheduling and Reusing Posts	46
Emailing students	47
Making Assignments in Google Classroom	47
Assignments in Google Drive	50
Student Assignment Views	51
Returning Assignments to Students	52

CHAPTER 5: HOW TO GET ANOTHER STUDENT OR A TEACHER INTO THE CLASS 56

Another Teacher Access	56
Adding Students	57
Guardian Access	59

CHAPTER 6: HOW TO MANAGE GRADES AND TRANSFER THEM TO GOOGLE SHEETS 62

Grading in classroom	62
Setting Points	63
Shared Doc is Best Way	63
Shorthand Grading	64
Auto Grade Questions	64
Decimal Grades	64
Grading Assignments	65
YouTube Feedback	68
Doctopus and GeoRubric	68
Commenting on Grades	69
Transfer grades to Google Docs and Google Sheets	71

CHAPTER 7: MOTIVATIONAL TECHNIQUES TO HELP KIDS GET EXCITED 74

Set your goals	74
Create a wonderful environment	75
Change the situation	75
Offers a variety of experiences	75
Use positive competition	76
Offer gifts	76
Encourage teamwork	76
Student chair	77
Try to maximize eye contact.	78

- MAKE SURE STUDENTS FEEL COMFORTABLE WITH EACH OTHER 78
- THINK IN ADVANCE HOW YOU INTEND TO ORGANIZE THE MODIFIED MEMBERS OR GROUPS 78
- ERROR CORRECTION 78
- USE RULES, FLASHCARDS, STORIES, AND TUTORIALS 79
- STUDENTS MUST BE RESPONSIBLE 80
- ASK STUDENTS TO WORK TOGETHER 80
- BET IF YOU WORK 81
- ENCOURAGE SELF-EXAMINATION 81
- USE IDENTITY AND RECOGNITION 81
- USING AUDIO AND VIDEO CONTENT: CASSETTE PLAYERS, VIDEOS, COMPUTERS 82
- INCREASE STUDENT INCENTIVES 83
- GIVE STUDENTS A SENSE OF MANAGEMENT 84
- DEAL WITH STUDENT ANXIETY 84
- USE STUDENT INTERESTS 84
- HELP STUDENTS FIND PHYSICAL MOTIVATION 85
- CREATE CURIOSITY 85
- TEACH YOUR STUDENTS TO ASK QUESTIONS 85
- BUILD LIFE EXPERIENCES OUTSIDE OF SCHOOL 86
- PERSONAL RESPONSIBILITY MUST BE DEVELOPED 86
- USE COLLABORATION 86
- STRENGTHEN COMMUNICATION BETWEEN INDIVIDUALS 87
- BIDDING OPTIONS 87
- USE THE CHANGES 87
- YOU CAN CREATE NOBLE GOALS, BUT THEY ARE ACHIEVABLE 88
- MAKE COMMENTS AND IMPROVE YOUR OPTIONS 89
- TRACK YOUR PROGRESS 89
- MAKE EVERYTHING FUN 89
- GIVE YOURSELF A CHANCE TO SUCCEED 89

CHAPTER 8: EXTENSIONS, HIDDEN FEATURES AND USEFUL APPS TO HELP STUDENTS SUCCEED 92

- GOOGLE CLASSROOM EXTENSIONS 92
- GOOGLE CLASSROOM APPS 106
- ADDITIONAL FEATURES IN THE GOOGLE CLASSROOM 114
- NEW FEATURES WITH GRADEBOOK 121

CONCLUSION 124

Introduction

With Google Classroom, a joint effort is simpler outside of school (i.e., Flipped Classroom). Once more, it's Cloud-based and open from anyplace with an association. Understudies can share assignments and work from home together to finish them. A coordinated effort isn't simply restricted to working in a gathering with different friends. A teacher can flip the classroom by sharing a video to go live at night, expecting understudies to see it that night to get ready for a test on it the following day. The conceivable outcomes are unfathomable.

Google Classroom is going to change the face of education. For years, teachers have spent so much of their time both inside and outside the classroom, trying to find the best way to educate their students and provide feedback promptly. In addition to spending time in the classroom going through their lesson plans, they also were in charge of copying materials, grading papers and essays, administering tests. All of these took a long time to accomplish and could cut into the learning time for the students. Sometimes, to save time, teachers would pick the easiest options for learning, cutting out creativity, and some of the fun in learning.

The hardships were not just on the teacher. Students often had to keep track of papers from different classes, and in the clutter, they may miss out on important announcements or information about the assignments. Asking questions both inside and outside of class could be a chore as reaching teachers was not always the easiest. And while the teacher was busy trying to organize their lesson plans or finding time to grade papers, the students were missing out on valuable learning time.

Google Classroom is a free platform that can make education better for both the teacher and the student. Teachers can have all their classes in one place, assign homework, and send announcements and save a lot of time. Students can always be up to date on their work, receive feedback on their assignments, and even reach their teacher in real-time. It is a win-win for both parties and can make learning fun and enjoyable again.

By the end of this, you will be looking at Google Classroom and will totally understand why it is an important one, and why you should always consider adding this to your repertoire of different items to try out in your classroom. Whether you're a new teacher looking for something new to use with your students, or a teacher who has been in the business for a while and might be hesitant upon using this system, everyone can benefit from this if you use this system. Ultimately, you'll be able to create the best and most worthwhile system that is out there, and that is offered.

You can use Google Classroom to your advantage in many different classroom environments, and you will learn from here why it is one of the best ways to engage your students, and why it matters.

The way forward for education is the digital and online way, and Google Classroom is one of the best purveyors of this new technology. Teachers, educators, and anyone wanting to share knowledge can use Google Classrooms as a way of teaching as well as learning.

CHAPTER 1:

The benefits of Google Classrooms

Exposes both Teachers and Students to Online Learning

Google Classroom is a great way to actually understand how to work in an online environment, and by being exposed to it early on, it allows for them to not be as shell-shocked when they finally make their way to college and realize that they'll have a lot of classes similar to this in the future.

Super easy to Get Materials

It's also super easy to access the materials, but this is good because no matter where they end up, they'll get the materials. Absent students can get the classroom materials from home if needed by simply logging in and getting the assignments by clicking on this. Gone are the days of having to deal with students having to chase after you just to get assignments.

All Work is There

One thing that's super annoying and frustrating for teachers is the fact that some students have a knack for losing work. Well, Google Classroom nips that in the bud. How? Well, it takes out that external document, and instead, everyone works in Google drive. Google Drive saves everything immediately, regardless of if you make one change to add a word, or if you work on the assignment for hours on end. It's super nice, and it saves you a lot of headaches. It's all there, and students never have to worry about "accidentally" losing work.

Creates Collaborative Learning

Because everything is digital, you can share content with peers in one single document that can be edited together, and then share another version for the students without the editing to this. If you want to, you can create assignment worksheets that are different for teachers and students, and from there, drive together with a question and answer system, and even create more in-depth discussions. It allows teachers to really engage with students. With the way technology is bringing everyone together, it's no wonder why teachers want to integrate this further and further into the classroom.

Students Take Ownership

One thing that teachers try to help students get better at is trying to stay more engaged in their studies. Well, Google Classroom can help with this. It is not just students reading and commenting on answers that the other students may have, it is also being in charge of their homework. Students can learn a subject they're having trouble with a little bit better if they are struggling with it, and in turn, if they want to utilize additional resources on their won, they can. The best part of Google Classroom is really just hos students can take charge of their learning environment, and in turn, create the best learning experience that they can.

Openness

Google Classroom can be gotten to from any PC through Google Chrome or from any cell phone paying little heed to stage. All records transferred by educators and students are put away in a Classroom envelope on Google Drive. Clients can get to Classroom whenever, anyplace. Students no longer need to stress over slammed PCs or hungry pooches.

Paperless

Educators and students won't have over the top measures of paper to rearrange since Classroom is paperless. At the point when educators transfer assignments and appraisals to Classroom, they are at the same time spared to Drive. Students can finish assignments and evaluations legitimately through Classroom, and their work is likewise saved to Drive. Students can get to missed work because of nonappearances and find different assets they may require.

Lifehack

Homeroom is a gigantic efficient device. With all assets spared in one spot and the capacity to get to Classroom anyplace, educators will have all the more leisure time to finish different errands. Since Classroom can be acquired from a cell phone, educators and students can take an interest through their telephones or tablets.

Differentiation

Through Classroom, teachers are effectively ready to differentiate guidance for learners. Allocating exercises to the entire class, singular understudies, or gatherings of understudies makes only a couple of straightforward strides when making a task on the Classwork page.

Criticism

Giving important input to understudies is a significant piece of all learning. Inside the reviewing apparatus of Classroom, teachers can send input to every understudy on assignments. The capacity to make a remark bank for some time later is likewise accessible inside the reviewing instrument. What's more, the Classroom portable application permits clients to comment on work.

Information Analysis

To make learning significant, teachers ought to examine the information from appraisals to guarantee understudies understand learning goals. Information from evaluations can undoubtedly be sent out into Sheets for arranging and investigation.

CHAPTER 2:

How to start a plan book for your class

Create a Lesson

When you teach using Google Classroom, your assignments become so much more than simply worksheets and projects. The ability to directly attach supplemental materials, videos, links, or other information lets you create comprehensive lessons and share them easily with your students.

To create an assignment, go into the class stream. Hover over the "Add" button at the bottom, then click "Create Assignment." You'll be prompted to enter a title and description or instructions. Whatever your title, the assignment will also be the name of the associated Google Drive folder, so make sure it's something you'll be able to easily find. Numbering your assignments can sometimes be a good idea.

You have a lot of options when you create an assignment. You can have it post immediately, save it as a draft, or finish it and schedule it to post at a later date. To post it immediately, click "Assign." For other options, click the down arrow beside it. Your scheduled posts and drafts will be in the "Saved posts" menu. You can choose the due date or set it to have no due date if you prefer. If you want to get very specific, you can even set the due date for a particular time.

You can also choose whether you assign it to an entire class or just to select students, which makes it easy to give out make-up work or follow-up revisions. The default will be to post to the entire class; to change this, click the down arrow next to "All students" then de-select the option. You'll now be able to choose which students receive the assignment.

Adding links or materials to your assignment is also easy. To upload a file, simply click "Attach," then select the correct file. You can add files both from your computer and from a Google Drive. If you want to remove the attachment, just click the "X." You can also attach links to videos or webpages that students should use as references.

When you upload a file, you'll have three options of how students can interact with it: view only, edit, or create a copy. The first is best for reading assignments and other materials the students should reference but not change. The last is best for worksheets and other assignments that students will fill out and post online, letting each student interact with his or her own assignment without impacting anyone else. The middle option is great for collaborative projects, and is very helpful for group or team projects, as will be described later in the book.

You can edit an assignment at any time by clicking on the three-dot "More" menu, then "Edit." Make your changes and save it as you would in any document. Keep in mind that if you've posted the same assignment to multiple classes, editing it will only affect a single class, not every assignment in every class.

After you've assigned the lesson, you can see how the students are interacting with it by clicking on the class, then on the assignment in question. The "Student Work" page lets you review how many students have completed the work at a glance and determine who still needs to turn in their project. You can also see who you've given feedback to, and view both the work and all comments on it by clicking on the student's name.

When you're interacting with students on an announcement or group-wide assignment, you can add either class comments or private comments for a single student. To make a comment private, click on the student's name, to comment to the whole class, click "Instructions," then "Add class comment."

The student view of all this will look different than what the teacher sees, of course. On their class stream, the assignment will have an "Open" button that will allow them to retrieve and then turn in the assignment. You may find it helpful to include instructions on how to interact with assignments in the class stream on the class' About page, especially for students who have limited experience with digital classrooms.

Google Forms

Most of us are familiar with Google tools like Drive and Docs, but those aren't the only free tools the company has that can be handy for teachers. If you're not familiar with Google Forms, you might be surprised by all the ways you can utilize them in your classroom to encourage collaboration, gather information about your students, and speed up your assessment process.

It is much easier to use Google Forms with Classroom than it used to be. When you make a post, you can attach a form using the Google Drive option. Students you share the post with will be automatically linked to a live version of the form. The teacher interface will also offer a link to view the results of the form in a convenient Google Sheet.

You'll need to create your form first before you make the post on Classroom. You can do this straight through Google Drive by clicking on the "New" button, then choosing the three-dot "More" menu and looking for Form. To navigate directly, you can instead go to forms.google.com. When you create a form, you have the option of using either multiple choice or open-ended answer formats. Enter your questions and save it, then navigate back to the Classroom interface.

You'll be able to link to the form you've created in the attachments option, under the "Google Drive" icon. Unlike other attachments, you won't be able to view or edit the form directly in the classroom. After the form is posted, clicking on it will open the editing screen for teachers, while it will open the form to be filled out for students.

Once a student has filled out the form, it will be marked as done in their assignment list automatically if the form is the only file in the assignment. If there are also other documents or links, the student will need to manually mark the assignment as finished by clicking in the lower right corner.

As students answer the quiz, teachers will be able to see all of their answers in one place on a searchable and sortable spreadsheet. You can then filter the results to see one student's answers, or all the students' answers to a particular question, giving you easier and deeper insight into the results.

Using Classwork

Creating content

Content creation in teaching is within the purview of making academic materials and study guides. The same applies to Google Classroom, which uses content in the form of text and attachments.

To accurately organize content relevant to a class, one must be able to follow the curriculum for the subject being treated. The modules and lessons employed for creating the course outline are what bring about flow and synergy in courses.

The same organizational strategy can be applied to content used in Google Classroom classes. The two tools used for this purpose are the topics and materials.

Topic

The foundation for content creation and organization in a class are the topics. Topics are created in tandem with other tools under Classwork. Hence, assignments, quizzes, questions, and materials are how topics are used in the Classroom.

After creating topics under different Classwork tools, you can then group the various posts under each Topic and arrange in a manner that allows proper flow of knowledge. Topics themselves can then be arranged in an order that flows with your curriculum. Posts not categorized under any topic stay at the top of the log unclassified.

Topics can be created directly under the Classwork menu. Select the create icon and select Topic to add a new topic. The topics you create are only visible to you; students only see topics with posts under them. For past unclassified posts, you can edit them and add the respective Topic.

Topics go hand-in-hand with materials, both make up the learning tools of the Classroom. Other tools under Classwork are for assessment. To add materials under their respective topics, go to Classwork, locate the Material, and click edit under more options. Toggle the topic dropdown from No topic to the appropriate Topic, you can create Topic or select a pre-existing one.

You can easily navigate Classwork posts under each Topic using the topic filter. Select the Topic dropdown and change from All topics to any topic to see the posts under the Topic. To order your Classwork tab, you can arrange the topics by moving them up or down. Drag a topic or select move up or move down under more options. When an item is moved, all posts under it are moved along.

After arranging by topics, you can then arrange the posts under each Topic. Do this by dragging items up or down directly or by using the move up or move down option. After all, you can edit the Topic itself if there is an error. Change the topic name by selecting more options next to the topic name tab, then select rename before saving.

Materials

Class materials are about the most crucial tools for learning in Google Classroom. With materials, there are no assignments, just informative items that can be read, watched, or listened to for a proper grasp on the topic being discussed.

Relevant materials for each Topic are posted under the Classwork section for students to have access to them. As we have said before, materials are like the lessons, while topics function as the modules for the online course.

The diversity of materials that can be posted in Google Classroom is another applaudable feat beneficial to learners made available. From text files to audio Material, video lessons, articles, textbooks, published books, web pages, and many more. The convenience Google Classroom offers when it comes to sharing files traces back to the use of Google Drive; files you upload once can be added to as many other classes using the drive link.

To add a material, go to Classwork under the Class you want to add the resources. Select Create and select Material to go to the editing page. Title and describe the Material in the fields provided, respectively.

At this stage, you can then add all the materials you wish to share with your students as attachments. Attachment options include google drive files, external webpage links, YouTube videos, and locally saved files on your personal computer.

To add google drive files, select the drive icon, then select add, which takes you to your google account drive folder. There, you can navigate to the choice file and choose the file to add as an attachment. For files you do not have permission for, you can simply make a copy which duplicates the file and adds to your Class google drive folder.

For adding YouTube videos, select the YouTube icon which pops up a search box and a link icon. You can search for relevant videos relating to your Topic by using keywords for your search. After getting your video of choice, click add to attach. On the other hand, if you have the video already, copy its URL and add it by pasting in the field prompt after selecting the URL icon.

For items sourced from any webpage, copy the webpage link, select the link icon and paste, then click add a link. For local system file uploads, select the file icon, browse through your system files and choose your choice file, then select upload.

The other option for adding attachments is to create a novel material using available google tools. This is a rather personalized option for getting materials across to students. You can add content specific to your Class like class notes, experiment results, survey statistics, and other vital information peculiar to your class students.

You can add written content using any of google docs, sheets, slides, drawings, and forms. Select the create icon on the materials page to add your preferred file type. A blank file is created and saved in the corresponding class drive. From here, you can edit the file as much as you want. The advantage of this form of material sharing is you can edit the files without having to go through the material page to reupload.

After adding all items, you are left with sharing the materials with the appropriate audience. Using the for dropdown, you can select which classes you want the Material shared. And with the All student's dropdown, you can decide to share only with a group of students belonging to the same Class.

Before posting a material, make sure to select the corresponding Topic from the No topic dropdown, you can as well create a topic if it isn't available yet. The Material can then be posted or scheduled for a later time using the post dropdown. There is also an option to save drafts for incomplete materials.

Any form of Material can be edited, whether posted, scheduled, or saved drafts. Locate the Material on the Classwork page, select the more options icon, then edit. After editing, select the appropriate status, post, schedule, or save a draft to keep your Material updated.

CHAPTER 3:

How to create a class and organize it

Step by step instructions to Create a Class

1. Navigate to https://classroom.google.com

2. Choose the "I am a Teacher" alternative

3. Click the "+" sign in the upper right-hand corner close to your Google account

4. Select "Make Class," at that point, give it a name and a segment, and snap "Make."

The "Segment" field is an optional descriptor for your group, so here you might need to include something like the first period, evaluation level, or some other short portrayal.

Customize the Appearance of Your Class

From the moment you make the class, we will have the possibility to insert a default header image. This is the image that students will see when they click on your group to get to their homework and statements. You can edit this image with a couple of quick steps.

1. Hover your mouse over the pennant picture

2. Look for the Select Theme connect in the base right-hand corner

3. Click Select Theme to open a display of photographs you can decide for your group.

4. Choose a picture from the display. At that point, click Select Class Theme to change your header picture.

Step by step instructions to Add Students to Google Classroom

Move, Edit or Archive a Class

1. Click the menu button in the upper left-hand corner of the screen (it would seem that three even lines)

2. Select Classes to see the entirety of the classes you have made

3. Now snap the three specks in the upper right-hand corner of the course you need to adjust

4. Choose Move, Edit or Archive to roll out the improvements you need

The Edit catch will let you rename your class or change the area, subject, or room number. The Move button permits you to adjust the request for the courses in your dashboard. The chronicle catch will expel the class from your dashboard and file it. At the point when a class is documented, you can, in any case, get to it through the Settings by tapping on the menu symbol in the upper left-hand corner and choosing Archived Classes. From here, you can reestablish chronicled classes or erase them for all time.

Homeroom Communication

There are two different ways to empower discourse among students and educators in Google Classroom. The first is the Stream - a Facebook-like mass of messages that can be seen by all individuals of the class. This element is accessible to the two students and instructors.

The following method to convey is by utilizing email. Students can tap the three dabs close to their educator's name on the class landing page to open a Gmail message that is auto-filled with their teacher's email address.

Students can likewise email each other by tapping the Students tab and tapping on the three spots to one side of the student's name and choosing Email Student.

Educators can do a similar when they click on the "Individuals" tab, be that as it may, they have the extra choice of choosing different students and afterward clicking Actions > Email to make an impression on a gathering of students.

Organizing Class Topics

To do this, you need to go to class-work, and then under the section, press the create button, and then you can choose a topic.

From there, whenever you add anything new, you can put a topic on it.

You can do this with assignments as well, that is already neatly put together as needed.

The Classroom Folder

If you're a teacher who isn't sure whether or not you've given a class a certain assignment, you can check the class folder.

It's located right on the home page of where the classes are listed. You can check the class folder in the Google drive.

If you want to easily ensure that you have a good organization system for the students as well, you can simply make folders for all of the students at this point, and then throw the work into there each time it's put in.

That way, you've got a great system and one that works correctly for you, no matter what the odds may be.

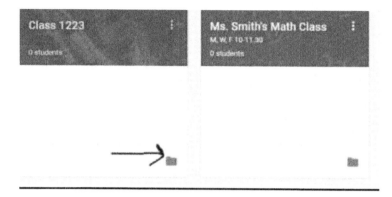

Commenting

Commenting is another big part, and it's mostly seen in the stream, or perhaps in a question that you assign. You can have two types, the class comments, and the private comments. Class comments you see under every single post that's there, and you can see all of them usually just by clicking on it. With the assignment, as you see how many are done/not done, you'll be able to look at comments, and you, as the teacher, can provide comments as needed, simply by clicking the reply option under the student's comment.

Now, if needed, you should use private comments. These are comments that are only seen by teachers, and they're available on assignments and questions. On the teacher's side, you can go to student work, choose a student, and from there, read a comment. You can then respond to it accordingly, based on what you need to say.

For students, you can go to any assignment, and at the bottom left corner, you can then add a private comment. The teacher can then get back to the student whenever possible and give the help they need.

For many teachers and students, knowing how to effectively create assignments is a great thing. It's so simple, since teachers can just make them in the drive, submit them to the classroom, and then students can put the work in. If needed, the teacher can step in and give help, and announcements and posts are there to help the students improve their learning experience. With all of this put together, it's a simple, yet very effective way to easily create the best classroom experience that you can and do what you feel is right to help your students better understand Google Classroom.

Announcements

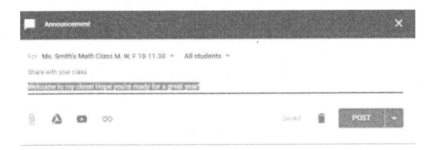

Announcements are great ways to communicate general information to the class, whether it be saying hello, making sure to remind them of something, or even giving them some information to help them better understand a project or subject in class. To do this, you need to press the plus sign on the right corner, and when you're given options, choose the option to create an announcement. From there, you can attach files using the paperclip option once again or even use various links to sources that you've found. It's quite easy, and it certainly does the job.

Lots of teachers like the announcement system, and students can comment on there to an announcement that they see unless you've turned it off. Students can also use it to communicate with you. If you're just now getting used to using it, you should use it as an introductory device. You can put a welcome announcement, have the students comment, or just write how you're excited to be their teacher this year. You can also tell students that commenting is super helpful for this and that they should be able to easily use it, and learn how to master this system.

CHAPTER 4:

How you can manage the due dates, homework, and assignments

Organizing Students Projects

While Google Classroom allows each student to attach multiple artifacts during submission of works, they can now submit all the pieces in one place and have it properly organized for the benefit of the teacher.

Projects can be set according to assignment options

For full class projects, send assignments to the entire class

You can send assignments to multiple classes by selecting the names of the classes you want to see the assignment before you send it

You can send the assignment to certain individuals to create specific student projects. When creating the assignment, do the following:

Deselect all students

Select the students that you want to be working on the specific project

Send the assignment

Only the individual students you selected will receive the assignment

You can send specific assignments to specific individuals by following the same steps as above

All the assignments will be organized by students' names, making it easier to keep on top of the assignments and grading.

The Google Classroom allows the teachers to create assignments and assign them to students. When working assignments, the teachers are provided with several options. The following steps will help you create an assignment in Google Classroom:

Begin by opening the class in which you need to create the assignment.

On the class page, click the CLASSWORK tab located at the top.

You will see a button written CREATE. Click this button.

After clicking the button, you will see many options showing the items that you can create for the class. Choose "Assignment".

A new window will pop up on which you should feed the details for the class. Give a title to the assignment as well as any additional instructions in the next box.

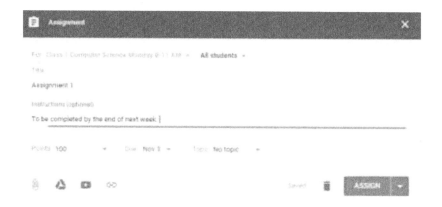

Note that the window also allows you to specify the due date for the assignment as well as the time on the due date by which the assignment should be submitted.

You are also allowed to choose the type of assignment that you need to create. It can be an assignment to all students or to just a selected few of them. You are also allowed to attach files to your assignment. Note that you can get these files from various storages, including Google Drive, your computer, *etc.* The file can also be a video file.

Once you have filled in all the assignment details, click the "Assign" button to assign the assignment to your students. Once the assignment has been created successfully, you will be notified of the same.

In some cases, you may need to assign the assignment to 1 class. In such a case, you only have to click on the class name from the top left corner of the window and choose all the classes to which you need to assign the work.

Most teachers who use the Google classroom will prefer to create an assignment from their Drive because this is where most teachers store their resources. However, you will get an advantage when you choose a Drive resource in the Google Classroom, which becomes clear with the options that you get when choosing a file from the drive:

Students will be able to view the file-you should only choose this option when you need all students to be in a position to view the file, but not to modify it. It is a good option for generic handouts and study guides that the entire class needs access to.

Students can edit the file-this option should be chosen when you need all students to be able to edit and work on one document. This is good for a collaborative class project in which the students may be working on different slides in a similar Google presentation. It is also well applicable in a situation where the students are all brainstorming on an idea collaboratively to discuss it in the next class.

Make a copy for each student-when this option is chosen, the Google Classroom will make a copy of the file for each student and give them the rights to edit the file. Note that only copies of the original file will be availed to the students, but the teacher's master will remain to him, and the students will not be granted access to it. This is a good option when you need to distribute a paper with an essay question for students to work on, or where you have a digital worksheet template that you need each student to fill their own answers.

You can also view your assignments at any time that you want. This is important as you may need to know the assignment details like the due date. This is possible, and it can be done by following the steps given below:

Sign in to your Google Classroom account.

Click the Menu button located at the top. Choose Calendar.

You will be taken to a new window with dates. To see either the past or future work, you must use the arrow that is next to the date.

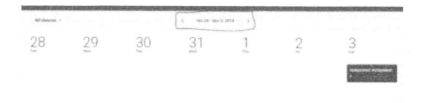

If you need to see all assignments for all your classes, just choose the "All classes" option. If you need to see the assignments for only one class, just click "All classes," then choose the class for which you need to see the assignments.

Once you identify an assignment or question that you are looking for, just click to open it.

How Students Access Assignments

When students log into their accounts, they can see their active assignments by clicking and opening the class that they are part of and viewing all their upcoming assignments. However, there is a quick and easy way to do this. Just click the Menu button located on the top left corner of the screen then choose "To-do" from the menu that pops out.

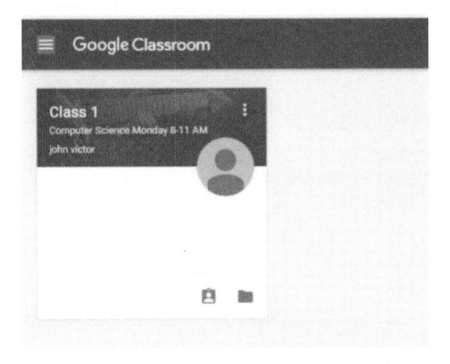

The student will then be able to see all the assignments for his or her classes as well as the ones they have turned in, the outstanding ones, and the overdue ones. The ones that the teacher has graded will be shown alongside their grades.

Once you click on any of the assignments, the relevant file for the student will be opened. If you are dealing with a Google Drive file, an additional button will be added to the toolbar located to the top right corner and close to the Share button. The button will be marked "Turn it in". Once you click the button, the assignment will be submitted to the teacher. For the regular assignment, you can submit by clicking the "MARK AS DONE" button.

Tips on Creating Differentiated Assignments on Google Classroom

Teachers using Google Classroom can transfer specific systems and methods that they use in the conventional classroom setting. When it comes to creating differentiated assignments, here are some tips on maximizing Google Classroom to reach your goal:

Focusing on the learning outcomes

Instead of emphasizing the directions for each assignment, teachers should focus on the results of each assignment. You want to push forth the learning concept that you want students to demonstrate. You can offer them several choices of how they can get this done, sort of like choosing your adventure to complete a quest. Make full use of the ability for commenting since students can privately speak to the teacher on an assignment, encourage them to write a comment to you on what approaches they can make and things that they can work on their assignments without revealing the content to other students.

Understand your learners

As a teacher, you already have a good idea of the various needs the students in your class has. Some students are ready for a challenge, whereas some need some handholding. When creating your differentiated assignments, a good thing to do is to look through your class roster and tick out which students fit with which assignment. Determine if these assignments can connect to their needs and appeal or excite them. Because Google Classroom enables you to add links from all over the web, make full use of it and add in a movie clip, a YouTube video, or a link to a website explanation. This gives the students a better idea of what kind of outcome you are expecting for each task.

Maintain motivation with different challenges

If you give a student too hard a task, they will most likely give up rather than persevere. Differentiating assignments allows students to understand a topic and complete assignments that they can grasp, and this will eventually help maintain the motivation within them until they finally reach the level on par with the rest of the class.

Leveling

If you are worried that your students may want to opt for tasks and assignments that are below their learning ability level, then you can also choose to code the assignments with levels. Coding assignment options can help a student choose the right task, just like how accelerated the reader assists the students in selecting books that are at their level of ability.

Tips for Managing Differentiated Assignments in Google Classroom

Number your assignments

Numbering your assignments and giving them specific names related to the student or group you want to send the assignment to is imperative so that you don't get confused. Include a number as well as an identifier for your own sake and sanity. The great thing about Google Classroom is that you can create as many assignments as you want, and all of these assignments will be shown in tiles format via a clean and intuitive design interface.

Make your directions specific

The more information you provide when creating these assignments, the fewer excuses you'd receive from students for not completing their tasks. Also, make your instructions easy to understand. Have sufficient information given but make it concise and easy to comprehend.

Utilize a rubric

A rubric will be able to make your students understand the end goal of the assignment and your expectations of the quality of the task. Include a rubric if you have one of those and make it clear what your expectations and outcomes are for the task.

Designate a group leader

Yup! Just like the conventional classroom setting, team leaders come in handy for group activities via cloud-based learning as well. The team leader is tasked with creating new files and turning them in through the Classroom for the entire group.

Student Submission of Assignments

The beautiful thing about Google Classrooms is the interaction that a student has with it as well. Students can turn in their completed assignments in a variety of ways, whether through a link, uploading a file to the Google Classroom, or retrieving it from Google drive. When you request your students to upload their assignments, make sure to give a particular format for task uploading, which includes the assignment number and their name. Depending on the tasks, students can upload or send you their versions of assignment answers and solutions, whether it is a blog post, a recreation of a city in Minecraft, a YouTube link, and even an essay. All these things promote creativity in a student as opposed to the conventional paper format of writing and submitting answers and turning in assignments.

Teachers can accept a variety of different outcomes to assignments because Google Classroom collates all this information in one place for each student submission for a particular assignment. For example, for assignment A, students are required to link/post/upload or save an assignment for the Assignment A folder. If a student were to email a teacher to submit their work, their email could get easily lost. The teacher would also have a hard time looking for it as well as categorizing the assignment.

Privacy

Student's submission is not publicly available for all other students to see. In a conventional classroom setting, it is very easy to know which student submitted what, especially if each submission is a different thing altogether. Via Google Classroom, students with alternative answers and options will be able to send in their assignment in privacy and not have to worry about being called out in front of the whole class.

Scheduling and Reusing Posts

Scheduling and reusing posts is something teachers do, especially if they have an assignment they liked. To schedule a post, you can create it so that it appears at a specific time and date. To do this, you press the option to create a post or assignment, and then on the side, you'll see a tab that has a plus sign on it. Press that, and you'll then be given the option to schedule it. From there, you can put in when it should appear on the stream, and it will happen. You can then finish up, and there you go. This is great for teachers who don't want to have to spend copious amounts of time scheduling.

Emailing students

Some teachers like to email students instead of just commenting on streams and such. If that's the case, you can go to the students tab. Usually, they show the names, and you can choose the student/s to email, and then you'll see three dots, which from there gives you the action to email students. Students can email the teacher by going to the three dots next to the name of the teacher, and from there, Gmail will open automatically, and the teacher's email address will be in there. They can also go to the students' tab, choose the student, and then go to the three dots and choose to email the student. This is not an ideal way to communicate, but it's one way to do so.

Making Assignments in Google Classroom

Making assignments and homework is a huge part of any teacher's job. Did you know that they are pretty simple to make, though? The first thing that you'll want to do when you title these is to always make sure that you have a number on them, such as 001, if you're going to have over 100 assignments for the class. This is super important since this makes it easier for students to find the assignment in Google Classroom, and it's okay since it'll give you a chance to create an order in case you accidentally assign something out of order.

Now to begin, you need to go to the class that is to get the assignment, and from there, go to the plus sign that you see, and you'll be given the option to create an assignment.

You'll see immediately that you've been given a header. Do think carefully about this, since as soon as you assign it, you'll see a folder created for it, and the title of it matches the header, so definitely be mindful of mistakes.

Now from here, you essentially give a description of the assignment and make sure that this is long enough for the student to go back to later if they missed it.

You can also choose the due date for it. You essentially choose the date it's due, and it also gives you the time option if you want it by a certain time on a certain date.

Now another big part of these points. Lots of classes do the point system, and it's a massive part of many curriculums, and this can be changed. You can assign a point value to it by adding in manually how many points you want to add, or if you want it to be un-graded, you can use the drop-down menu to change it.

Finally, you've got the chance to add attachments. You can create templates in Google drive then add them here, and the student can then fill them out. You can give links to students, too if you want them to use a link to fill out the assignment they have.

If you want to assign this to multiple classes, you choose the class near the top, and then all of the classes to assign the work to.

Assignments in Google Drive

When using Google Classroom, sometimes teachers create assignments from the drive. For example, maybe there's a worksheet that can be used that they scan and put on the drive itself. This is actually how the resources are kept for teachers. Now, when you have an assignment that you want to put on there, you essentially need to go to Google Drive and make sure that you choose the right option. That's because you get three different choices, and they are as follows:

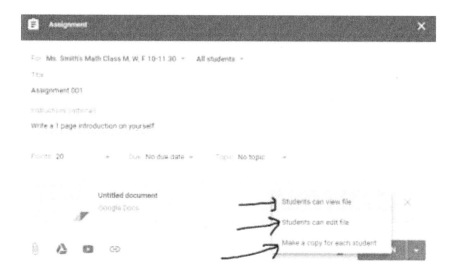

Within these options, you get the following, and these appear every time you put a Google document on there:

Students can view the file: basically, means they can look at it but aren't allowed to modify, as in the case of study guides and handouts

Students can edit the file: this is where they can edit the document and then work on it, which works for collaborative projects that students do together, such as various projects that they do, including group projects. Slides for an assignment are good for this too, or where they put together brainstorming ideas

Make a copy: this is a way where you can choose to make a copy of the file for every single student, and they get individual editing rights for it. The master is intact, and students can't access it, but they get to fill out the other one, and this is good for any assignments that involve filling out questions, or worksheets, and such.

If you're wondering whether or not you should assign it to a few or too many, this is a good option.

Student Assignment Views

For students, it's a bit different, since they will see a different view compared to teachers. Essentially, they see the description for the assignment, and in it, a button that says open, which is where the

student will put the assignment. Make sure you inform the students that they need to choose whether they are marking it as done or turning it in, depending on if they have to turn in anything or not.

Returning Assignments to Students

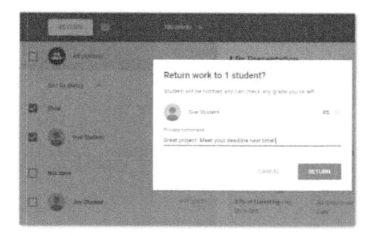

Assignments can be returned to the student at this point by pressing the box that says, return. You can return it before it's recorded. When it's recorded, it's done with. You can then press the option to return the assignment.

Now, if you have additional feedback, it'll give you an option to do that too. Again, it's ultimately up to you. If you have no feedback, don't worry about that part. If you do have more feedback, then throw it in quickly before it's completely returned to the student. Remember, it's better to be a bit overboard with grading if you have feedback that will help students become better, and to help them understand the subject at hand.

Tips

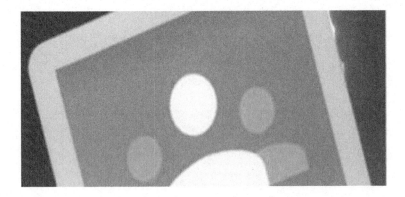

The first tip is that when you're making assignments, don't use MS Word. Instead, use the Google drive apps, since they are completely integrated with the classroom system. If you do use a Microsoft Word file, the student will have to download the files once more, upload them again, and then attach them. You will also need to put in the extra work with downloading and reattaching, and it's just a lot of extra fluff that you don't need. The drive files are there for a reason, and they're super easy to create. However, if you export a sheet from MS Word to drive, it works the same way, making it easy for everyone.

Another helpful tip is that you can actually use shortcuts to add comments. You can use control alt and then M to put comments into a document on Google docs. You can then press the enter key to close the comment, and control plus W to actually close the document itself. You can also do feedback by choosing the name of the students, and then looking at the options to see what they've submitted. You can go to the add private comment section on this, and also enter grades for students. You can't actually get a grade book with Google Classroom, just notify students of the grades.

With Google Classroom, the key way to ensure that you're getting feedback to students quickly is through adding the mobile app. It allows you to add comments to various projects, and answer questions on grades. Plus, it's integral if you want to make sure whether a student got the assignment or not.

Another important tip is to utilize the form templates to help with grades. The form template can be used to make a sheet with the names, and a checklist of various elements, including what they're missing, homework points, and other elements. By carrying this around, you can also grade the students, and it's good to have if you want to check out whether or not they have their homework done.

Another really cool tip is that if you want to make your grading faster, it is possible to use shorthand. Google docs know immediately what you're saying, so if you use shorthand, and you type in the letters "wc" it will automatically change this to word choice, which will communicate to the students that it's bad word choice. It makes your life so much easier, especially if you're going through grading multiple papers.

It's also important for teachers to remember that when you give an assignment back, you can't edit it anymore. That means that if you need to edit anything else, they will need to resubmit it. You can notify them, and they can look at it, and if they resubmit it with changes, and you edit it, and it's all good, you can also edit the grades by looking at the grade, pressing it, and then choosing the option to update the grade.

CHAPTER 5:

How to get another student or a teacher into the class

Another Teacher Access

To give other teachers access to your Google Classroom class activities, you need to enable individual permissions, and they, on their end, would accept the invite.

Inviting a co-teacher to join your class gives them access to perform all functions of a teacher on your class page. They can post in the Stream, leave comments, assign work and topics, and even grade students. They are there to help your work in totality.

However, there are only a few permissions that distinguish the class owner from the sharing teacher. Such as the site of the class' google drive folder, present with the primary teacher, and only shared with the co-teacher.

Inviting teachers is also moderated by G-suite administrators. Such that only Classroom accounts with the school's domain name can't be requested inherently. To invite a third party carrying a different mail pattern would require access from the admin's end.

For co-teachers, there is an option to invite individual teachers or a group of teachers. Each teacher in the class has the right to leave at any given time, except you as the primary teacher. To gain access again, any co-teacher that parts would have to be re-invited.

To invite teachers, navigate to "People" in the class menu for which you wish to add teacher participants.

Then select the "Invite teachers" option. You then have to provide the email addresses of the individual or group of teachers for invites to be sent.

For an invited teacher, when you log in to your Classroom dashboard, the requested class card shows a prompt to accept or decline the offer. And otherwise, an email notification is sent to invited teachers, and the offer can be received from there.

The co-teacher gets the option to leave an invited class almost as easily as they joined. Simply navigate to "Options" on the Class page or the "People page", then navigate to "Leave class" and select. After confirming the prompt, you are free to go.

Adding Students

The main target of the class is the students. Hence, a more dynamic approach is needed for gathering your students.

There are more available means for adding students than all of the other participants of a class.

Invitation from Teacher

This is an excellent method for populating your Google Class with your students. You can invite as many students as 1000 in groups or individually.

A readily available option is the email list provided by your school G-Suite administrator. The student email list is grouped based on common qualities like those at a given level or those taking a particular course. This helps administrators or class owners to invite students in bulk and get their classes populated easily.

Inviting students to join your class can as well be done under the "People" menu. After adding the respective email addresses and invites are sent out, students receive email notifications and can easily accept the invitation from email or by login to the Classroom homepage.

Sharing Class Code

The use of a class code is peculiar to adding students to a class. The code doesn't work for adding co-teachers or guardians. Using a code allows students the opportunity to create a Google Classroom account if they didn't have one.

The class code is on the class homepage just above the Stream. The code can be copied and shared or just shared as a link. Google classroom also allows for the code to be made full-screen and displayed over a projector.

To join a class using class codes, students log on to their Classroom account and select the "Add Class" icon. Then select "Join Class" to enter the code in the provided field. After submitting, the student immediately becomes a member of the class. After your class is filled with your students, you disable the code to prevent its abuse. The code can be switched back on at will when the need arises.

For students using a mail address different from the school's domain, they require special permission from the school G-Suite administrator to allow external domain accounts to join classes.

Guardian Access

The guardian report is an improvement to help parents and guardians monitor their ward's class performances. Access to Google Classroom for guardians is only available for G-Suite accounts and can only be granted by the account administrator or class owner.

The guardian report is set to a preferred frequency at which a summary of the student's activities in class is sent to the registered guardian account. Any email type can be invited since only email notifications need to be received.

Guardians need to submit their details with the school authority to fix to the appropriate classes their ward attends. The guardian receives a confirmation mail to accept the invitation to receive periodical reports on their ward's class activities. The summary contains information such as missing work, class activity, and even future work.

As a guardian, you can decline access to receiving a summary may be in situations where the student assigned isn't rightward. Also, you can remove yourself as a guardian at any time. And better still, if you operate a Google account, you can toggle the settings of the summary to determine when and how often you receive the roundups.

CHAPTER 6:

How to manage grades and transfer them to Google Sheets

Grading in classroom

Grading in the classroom is quite easy. The first thing you do is you go to the classes that you have and check out the assignments tab. From there, you can see who has and who hasn't completed it, and you can then click the number over those who have finished showcasing who has finished the assignment and turned it in.

From there, you can click the name of the student to see the document and then look at any documents attached to it. You can, from there, read it, grade it, and then close it and then go to the student work page.

You want to click on the person who had the assignment, and it will say no grade.

From there, you type in the point system, then press the checkbox, and then choose a return. Once returned, they are recorded, and the classroom will ask if you want to attach any further feedback. You can choose what to do there at your own discretion.

Setting Points

One cool thing about this is that you can choose how many points an assignment is now in Google classroom, which makes it much easier for grading. You can put the tally of points at the top now as you add or edit questions. This is done automatically, and it's part of a new update and machine learning. So, gone are the days of trying to calculate how many points something is or how many questions you can set it yourself., and Google will do the work for you, saving you lots of time.

Shared Doc is Best Way

If you are looking to quickly get feedback to the students quicker, always make a Google doc for shared assignments since that does provide quicker feedback when grading them. You can always choose to "add comments," and from there, add comments and feedback without changing the document within the classroom itself. You do not have to mark up pages in red anymore, but if you want to, you can still use red ink for correcting them, which is really nice. If a document is unfinished, and the student is asking you to give them a bit of feedback, you can go into these right away and see for yourself. What needs to be changed. In a similar vein, if you do use a Google form template for the skills and homework points, you can always change these as well, and if it's changed similarly, it allows for a teacher to quickly give feedback to students.

Shorthand Grading

You can actually use symbols and abbreviations to grade these, and if you correctly set these, the document will change these. You don't have to worry so much about writing down countless amounts of information, but instead, you can type in something as simple as "sp." Through machine learning, Google Classroom can change that and insert in there "spelling issues/wrongly spelled" without you having to type out so much. It looks better, and students will understand what you mean by that.

Auto Grade Questions

If you use grid-style questions or checkbox assignments, you can create the correct answers, and the quizzes will be auto-graded. It creates an easier system for teachers so that teachers don't have to ask the same types of questions and instead collect everything in a way that's smart and effective as well.

Decimal Grades

How awesome would it be to give partial credit on something in a simple, yet flexible manner? Well, now you can with your Google forms, and a recent update allows you to give decimal answers. For example, if the answer is half-right or maybe they are missing a part, you can now give half of a point, and that will allow for more exact grading.

You do not have to write a copious amount of notes categorizing half-right, or all-right and what went wrong. It allows for much more exact grading, which is super nice.

Grading Assignments

There are a different number of ways through which teachers can find submissions from students. The most effective way of doing it is by entering the class that you need to grade then click the name of the assignment from Stream view. If you find that the assignments get lost within the conversations being done by students, look at the sidebar located at the top left of the Stream view, and you will be able to see the box for "Upcoming Assignments".

The above figure shows that the student has already turned in the assignment. It is now the work of the teacher to assign student marks. You can see that the section for marks is assigned __/100.

Identify the assignment that you need to grade then follow the steps given below:

Click on the name of the student who submitted the assignment that you need to grade.

If the student had attached a document, it would be opened. You can rely on the commenting feature in Drive to give detailed feedback on the specific parts of the submission made by the student. Once done, close the document. The changes that you have made will be saved automatically.

After returning to the classroom, click the box to the right of the student name where it is written __/100. In my case, the total for the assignment is 00, and I want to assign 68 marks to the student. I simply type 68 inside that box. I should now have the following:

Ensure that you have checked the box located to the left of the student name then click the "Return" button located at the top of the window. This will save the grade that you have assigned the student. In addition to this, the student will be notified that the assignment they submitted has been graded. After clicking the RETURN button, a new window will pop up, asking you to confirm the return to the student.

If you have any additional comments to the student regarding the assignment, write them in the provided box. Click RETURN again, and the process will continue successfully:

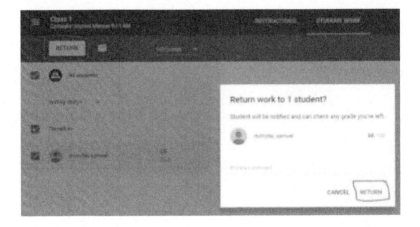

You will also see on the window on the left side the students whom you have graded. In my cases, I have assigned only one student a grade, as shown below:

The name of the student, as well as the grade assigned, is shown in the window.

YouTube Feedback

Some students learn better if they are given a video to better understand a concept. Instead of just trying to write it out twenty times in hopes they will understand, why not give a YouTube link to the issue they are struggling with. This is a super awesome means of helping students understand a concept that they don't totally grasp whenever you grade it. You can pair it with a link either to YouTube, WatchKnowLearn, Khan Academy, or other educational resources, which is perfect if a student is struggling with a concept and needs that little extra boost to help them understand the concept in a better manner.

Doctopus and GeoRubric

These are two beneficial apps for grading. Doctopus is an add-on to Google sheets, and it is a teacher-created tool that allows for managing, assessing, and organizing projects within Google drive. It mostly begins with a starter template that's mass copied, and from there shared. The same template can be used to manage the grades. Goobric is an instrument that can help create an effective grading rubric for the student's grades and will help with seeing as well just what the grades of a student are currently. By pairing this with Doctopus, you essentially will auto-fill out a rubric, and from there, Doctopus puts it onto a spreadsheet. It saves you a buttload of time trying to grade everything, and these two apps are both integrated with Google Classroom, which in turn will allow teachers to do a whole lot more with this and allow for a much more integrative and better learning system.

Grading assignments is a teacher's job, and while it may not be the most fun job out there, Google Classroom has made it way easier and simpler. With some of the new additions to this, it allows teachers to create a system that allows you to have a simple, yet effective sort of job that they will enjoy. When a teacher uses this, they will realize just how simple it is to integrate this into the classroom, and from there, they can facilitate grading and get the feedback that students want on their work. It creates a better, easier system, and it also gets teachers much more involved in their student's progress since they can keep track of what needs to be worked on, and what students are grasping easily.

Commenting on Grades

At this point, you're then opening it up in the drive and can start to comment, too. If you're a teacher who likes to grade with a red pen, for example, you can essentially go to the text button, change the color to red, and then comment. But it's a bit easier this time around. If you want to, you can use the feature that allows you to comment to give the appropriate feedback. To do this, you highlight what you're about to comment on, and then choose the option to insert, and then make your comment. When you've finished typing in what you need, save it, and it will be saved completely for the student. You can mark up the assignment as needed, or even leave positive comments if there is something the student did well with.

Now from there, you can go to the class-work tab, then the assignment name, and then view it. If you haven't changed the value of the point system yet, you can always change it. From there, choose the student file that you've finished, and enter the name, then the grade. It is then ready to be returned to the student for review.

However, if you want to change the grade itself, you can go to the assignment that the student has and then enter the grade. You can also return them ungraded as needed. Remember that the changes to the grade only affect those not yet returned, and original ones have the same grade as before.

Transfer grades to Google Docs and Google Sheets

Finally, let's talk about exporting grades. Grades can be exported, and they're used to make sure that you have a place for all of them. Remember, this just displays the grades and isn't a biodegrade, but if you want to help export them so that they're all written down, you can. Lots of teachers like to export them into a .csv file, or through Google sheets. With sheets, you can create an average for the class and for students, and actually set up arrows from one grade box to another one, which makes it faster.

To export these grades into sheets, you go to Google Classroom, choose your class, and then the assignments. From there, go to settings and choose the option to copy all of the grades into Google sheets. An automatic spreadsheet will then be created on the drive folder, allowing you to see all the grades. Currently, though, you can only export these on the desktop version of the classroom, not on a mobile version or via the app.

> Copy all grades to Google Sheets
>
> Download all grades as CSV
>
> Download these grades as CSV

Now, if you export these grades to a CSV file, you'll be able to have all of the grades in one place. This is good if you're trying to keep every single grade in one place, and if you want to print them out. To do this, you go to Google Classroom again, click on the class you want, then go to settings once again and choose an option, either to download the assignment grades for that one only or to download all of the assignment and question grades. For the first, you choose: download these grades as a CSV, and for the assignment and question grades, you choose: download all grades as a CSV. From there, you can find them in your downloads folder and can bring them up on your word processing device accordingly.

For many teachers, the element of grading is made so much more comfortable with Google Classroom, since they can easily create the environment that they want and set it all set up so that students can access it easily. It's easy and straightforward to achieve, so you'll be able to create the best and easiest classroom experience that they can possibly have.

A great feature of Google Docs for teachers is the ability to track changes made to a document by each of the participants using the Revision History feature.

CHAPTER 7:

Motivational techniques to help kids get excited

The word "motivation" is generally defined as the power that causes, selects, and follows the behavior. In fact, it is often used to describe certain types of behavior. A student who studies and tries to enter the upper class is considered "highly motivated", but a friend said he had "difficulty motivating". These statements show that motivation has a profound effect on our behavior.

Motivation can be defined as a term used to describe aspects of a person who raises, maintains, and guides goal-oriented behavior. Another way to do this is to say that motivation is intentional behavior.

Set your goals

It can be very frustrating for students to complete assignments or even be brought to class if there are no clear goals. Students want and need to know what they can expect to be motivated at work. At the beginning of the year, set clear goals, rules, and expectations for students so that they are not compromised, and students have goals to work with.

Create a wonderful environment

While students need to understand that their actions have consequences, they encourage students to be more than threats, positive reinforcement. When teachers create a safe and supportive environment for students by strengthening their confidence in students' abilities, rather than exposing the consequences of non-response, students are more likely to be motivated to work. In the end, students meet the expectations that the adults around them don't communicate, so focus on what you know and what you don't.

Change the situation

Classes are a great place to study but sitting at your desk every day seems a little boring for some students. To renew your interest in this topic, or merely general education, allow students to leave the classroom. Be willing to travel, bring a speaker, or even go to the study library. The brain likes innovation, and some approaches may require new approaches to stimulate learning.

Offers a variety of experiences

Not all students respond to lessons in the same way. For some people, the occasional experience may be the best. Others want to read books quietly or work in groups. To interest, all students combine their classes so that students with different choices focus on the time of their choice. So students continue to participate and pay attention.

Use positive competition

Competition in the classroom is not always a bad thing, and in some cases, it can encourage students to work harder and strive for excellence. Work in the classroom to encourage a friendly competitive spirit, perhaps group games that provide financial or other opportunities to show students their knowledge.

Offer gifts

Everyone likes to receive awards, and great motivation is to offer students opportunities. Things like pizza breaks, watching movies, or even simple things like climbing on paper allow students to work harder and achieve their goals. Consider the personalities of the students and the need to determine the appropriate rewards for the class.

Encourage teamwork

One successful way, if the teacher is active and able enough, is to encourage students to participate in classes by making appropriate use of "social work" or "teamwork". The language is best learned through close collaboration and student communication. This type of collaboration benefits all or both students. In fact, students can help each other when working on a variety of activities such as writing conversations, conducting interviews, drawing and commenting, interpreting roles, and so on...

Research on second language acquisition shows that students have different skills; while one student is well-drawn, the other students can communicate orally; third, students can play and imitate roles well. Also, some students, if they feel uncomfortable, are less stress-free when learning specific rules or languages from their aunts and friends than from the teacher. Finally, the language of communication requires togetherness and an environment of mutual trust and confidence that can be provided by "co-workers" or "teamwork".

Student chair

How students sit in the classroom often determines the dynamics of teaching. In fact, simply changing the layout of a session can greatly affect group cohesion and student satisfaction, and I have seen many other examples where sessions are important factors in successes or failures in learning. In some cases, this is not entirely in your hands, for example, if it is mounted on the floor, on the table or if the school has strict rules to avoid moving furniture. The number of students is also a problem.

I'm going to talk about the middle class - from the age of 6-25. The teacher has a variety of options for arranging the sessions - the groups sitting at the small table are often chosen. This is probably the best choice for a larger class in this area, but with smaller numbers and adult or teenage students, I think a horse outbreak, I noticed, has all the benefits of a group and has no flaws. The horseshoe can be a U-shaped plank with a middle hole, semicircular students, with chairs and tables without tables, or students sitting on three sides of a large table, with the teacher at the end. However, regardless of the type of seats selected or applied, the party is likely to be successful if you consider the following principles:

Try to maximize eye contact.

Teachers, pupils, and students, if the speaker does not come into visual contact with others, attention is usually reduced. This is the main reason why I personally think the horse shape is better.

Make sure students feel comfortable with each other.

Make sure none of your students sit alone or away from the group. Also, try to leave empty spaces, but not too much space, because large distances between students produce a "quiet" atmosphere, low speed, and less active participation in the classroom.

Think in advance how you intend to organize the modified members or groups.

This is part of the class, which can be a problem if students are not followed closely as they do not know where to go or transfer to a safe place.

Error correction

We always ask if we correct the mistakes of each student whenever they appear. The correct answer is that if we stop and treat all mistakes without avoiding mistakes, this will lead to a lack of communication and fear that students will make too many mistakes.

Therefore, because students are overloaded with mistakes, students become very willing to engage in research. Therefore, the teacher must understand when mistakes need to be corrected and how to act with deeds and do so without shame. In teacher-centered lessons, mistakes that are unconsciously corrected by students are best corrected when there is a lack of communication or mistakes are not resolved, leading to misunderstandings of the ideas created.

In terms of error correction, there are various methods that a teacher is believed to follow. The teacher should choose the type of error and plan if a wrong language form occurs. These adjustments include teacher self-correction.

Use Rules, Flashcards, Stories, and Tutorials

Reality cards and flashcards can be considered essential tools for learning foreign languages, with new sentences such as fruit, vegetables, clothes, *etc.* Play a useful role. Study. Otherwise, they are very useful, especially for beginners. Pay attention to follow and match new words in the article. In addition, the reality is an authentic material that helps teachers overcome craftsmanship in the classroom. Creating stories with students is another way to develop speaking and writing skills. Indeed, stories are made based on students' ability to create stories based on their personal experiences. Some problems arise when creating stories, for example, a) fluently, b) if students have enough language to make a story, and c) accuracy.

The teacher can demonstrate the use of different legal methods to learn grammar, vocabulary, pronunciation, and community structures in which students appreciate the law and encourage them to learn English in interesting ways. The teacher can stimulate students' ideas about songs through activities such as inhibition, ideas, dissemination, and so on. Students will discuss problems such as emotions, what will happen next, and more. And write the answer interestingly. Students can write and show how the song feels and thus attract their emotions when they listen to the song. The teacher will answer this presentation and ask questions. The group then provides feedback.

Students must be responsible

Distributing students' homework in the classroom is a great way to understand students' structure and motivation. Most students consider schoolwork a privilege rather than a burden and work hard to ensure that they and other students meet expectations. It can also help allow students to take the lead or help those who are important and appreciated by all.

Ask students to work together

Although not all students dance for opportunities in group work, many are willing to try to solve problems, experiment, and work with other students. Social communication can be rigorous for class objects, and students can encourage each other to achieve a goal. The teacher must make sure that the group is balanced and correct so that some students don't work more than others.

Bet if you work

There are no other motivations that work beyond motivation. Even as adults, we need recognition and praise, and students of all ages are no exception. Teachers can offer generous encouragement to students by publicly rewarding success, praising them for successful work, and sharing exemplary work.

Encourage self-examination

Most children need success, they just need help finding out what to do to reach them. One way to motivate students is to see them and identify their strengths and weaknesses. Students are often much more excited to organize such criticisms on their own than teachers because they force them to create their own goals.

Use identity and recognition

Students are best known for memorizing their names. Students must know that their interest as a teacher places them in a caring interest and success. When students are appreciated, it creates a safe learning environment. It encourages them to work harder because they want to receive good praise and feedback from people they believe they know and appreciate.

Acknowledgment/confirmation is only valid. "I know you did Homework,"encourages self-awareness and reflection. Consider repeating the comments you hear when someone tells you."Evelyn made interesting comments on what we explored. I think it needs to be repeated."

What has been achieved with this simple technology?

You give recognition.

Not only does it encourage Evelyn, but she also encourages others to get more involved.

He showed that he was open to feedback and that students' opinions could improve their learning.

Using audio and video content: cassette players, videos, computers...

Since our school is equipped with a range of audio and video media, such as recorders, videos, computers, designers, magazines, etc., teachers must use this material for their teaching. In fact, they need the right material that they can use to design their watches. For example, we must include a cassette player in the audio guides and include a computer in all electronic learning or design a lesson on the school website.

There are other reasons why the use of students' native languages emerged for historical reasons. First, it was part of the response to the method of linguistic translation that prevailed between the late nineteenth and early twentieth centuries, in which language teaching is seen as a means of intellectual development rather than as dogs in historical communication.

However, we can say that there are situations where we can use the student's native language, for example:

- If there is a lack of communication or a complete misunderstanding, as this could prevent wasting time explanations and, if possible, instructions unnecessary to deal with good language.

- It can be used in reverse to highlight the grammar of the problem.

For example, various textbooks, such as Headway, encourage students to translate exemplary sentences into their own language to compare and contrast grammar.

- It can be used for beginners when students try to say something but find it difficult to say it in their own language, and the teacher can translate it for them. - When students need to connect both languages, for example, in lessons focused on translation and interpretation.

Increase student incentives

The best lessons, books, and materials in the world do not involve students' interest in learning, and they are willing to work hard if they are not interested.

Internal and external motivation is the key to student success at all levels of their education, and teachers can play an important role in providing such motivation for students. Of course, this is easier said than done because all students are otherwise interested and require a lot of time to study in a classroom filled with children who are eager to learn, work hard and strive to achieve perfection.

Even the most advanced and talented teachers cannot turn children, whether you are a new teacher or a specialist, try this method to motivate and inspire students to use their true abilities.

Give Students A Sense of Management.

While teacher leadership is important in keeping children active and motivated, it is actually one of the best ways of engaging their students to choose and manage classroom events freely. For example, if students can choose the types of tasks, they need to do or the problems they face, they can give them a control check that can only motivate them to do more.

Deal with student anxiety

Some students fear they are not performing well and are worried about the predictions that they will perform themselves. Teachers of these students may find that they learn more enthusiastically if the struggle with content is not the end of the world. The support is independent of the end result and ensures that students do not rely too heavily on the expectations they provide.

Use student interests

There are several other benefits of getting to know students, which allows you to link classroom content to things that students are interested in or have experienced. Teachers can use this hobby to make things more interesting and relevant to motivate students and long-term students.

Help students find physical motivation

It can be amazing to help students motivate themselves, but ultimately they need to be able to create their own incentives. One of the most powerful gifts you can give them is to help students learn the personal reasons for doing classwork and hard work, whether they find interesting material, want to go to college, or study.

Create curiosity

Curiosity is perhaps the most exciting. Here is the difference between American and Japanese teaching styles: in Japanese schools, students are given problems or challenges, they discuss. Curiosity arises, of course. Instead, the main ideas are presented in U.S. schools, the solution is taught, and students are trained. Where does this curiosity come from?

Teach your students to ask questions

Encourage students to ask questions. The interrogation process starts the thought process. When students ask "Why?" and "How?" problems are growing, both awareness and interest. We probably answer only three questions: questions, phone, doorbell, and email.

Build life experiences outside of school

The theory is important, but the greater the interest in practice, it shows how learning makes life easier and better. Share how content helps students make better decisions, solve more problems, get to know others, and be more focused.

Personal responsibility must be developed

Remember the principle of encouragement: people encourage themselves consciously or unconsciously. Everyone is responsible for learning, but it is the teacher's responsibility to create the best possible atmosphere where learning can take place. An effective way to do this is to give students the opportunity at the beginning of the lesson:

What are their hopes?

What is the expected result?

What are they willing to do to achieve this result?

Use collaboration

Competition increases performance, not learning. Yes, some students practice for hours to encourage the spirit of competition, be it music, sports or the performing arts. But these students are encouraged to compete.

And competing for a short time can be a lot of fun, but very devastating for teenagers who have never competed with others before. Instead of competing, students give up by giving up. Each time a teacher asks for a group, students compete for the teacher's attention, and usually only one student works. A better way is to build a student partner. Even a timid student shares it with others. So instead of asking questions, ask questions. When asked for the correct answer, the writer calls for thought. Ask students to discuss each other's answers. With this method, all students participate.

Strengthen communication between individuals

Keeping in touch with students is valuable, but even more valuable in helping you build relationships. Give students a chance to spend a short time before learning activities begin. Building relationships between young people is very important.

Bidding Options

Everyone, regardless of age, loves control over their lives. When we can make decisions, we feel in control. Choose activities, and that includes homework. By offering two, three, or even four activities and allowing students to choose between them, teachers provide them with an opportunity for some encouragement.

Use the changes

Many visual technologies can be used, including illustrations; animation; the selected film, video and/or DVD section; PowerPoint works; and transparency. Some characters (teachers and/or students) dress well.

There are many audio technologies to use, such as playing music, recording music, writing poetry, or anything rhythmic. Do you remember how you studied your ABC? The song "Twinkle, Twinkle Little Star" is a "song of the alphabet".

Part of the kinetic energy can be used. Example: spelling words in the air, standing in small groups, intertwined with emotional illnesses like immigrants on a transatlantic ship, and with only five ways to attract attention (two eyes on the teacher, two ears for listening, one mouth closed).

Other methods include connecting large group discussions, case studies, and personal experiences with friends who are exploring the topic.

Another method is to use study materials for students who need to complete it during college. This feature always attracts me and gives them something to refer to later. This simple technology allows you to cover more content in a shorter period of time.

You can create noble goals, but they are achievable

Most people don't try to do it themselves unless they encourage students to do more than they should. Students want to challenge and strive to achieve high expectations as long as they feel they have achieved that goal, so don't be afraid to encourage students to achieve as much as possible.

Make comments and improve your options

Students struggling with classwork are sometimes frustrated, fall for themselves, and give incentives. In these situations, the teacher needs to help students learn exactly where they are wrong and how they can improve further. Understand three ways to find out how students want to help them be motivated to work hard.

Track your progress

It can be difficult for students to see that they have gone far, especially with heavy content. Monitoring can be useful in the classroom, not only for teachers but also for students. Teachers can use this to motivate students and allow them to see visually what they are learning and developing throughout the year.

Make everything fun

Not every class should be a game or a good time, but students who see the school as a playground are more interested in attention and doing the necessary work than those who are thinking about it. Thank you for your work. By providing fun activities throughout the school day, you can help the work of students who want to step forward and make the class more friendly to all students.

Give yourself a chance to succeed

Even the best students can be frustrated and deterred when they get into trouble or when they don't get recognition from other students.

Make sure all students have the opportunity to play according to their strengths and to feel involved and respected. You can make the world differently depending on your motivation.

CHAPTER 8:

Extensions, hidden features and useful apps to help students succeed

Google Classroom Extensions

With extensions, you and your students can have a better experience when using the Google Classroom. It is recommended that when using Google Classroom, use Chrome as your browser. Let us discuss some of the extensions that you can integrate with Google Classroom to have an improved experience:

Share to Classroom

This is a Chrome extension developed by Google, and it helps to save time when using Google Classroom. This extension will help you to push the web pages to any of your Classroom classes so that they can be opened instantly on the student's computers. It is a good extension for getting students on the right page more quickly and reliably. The extension will allow you to create assignments, post announcements, or save web pages that will be posted to the Classroom at a later time.

The share to classroom extension is available for teachers that use either laptops or chrome books within the classroom, and this extension allows teachers to show the screens and work within the class, so teachers can share websites to the computer. They can essentially click on the extension, and from there, choose to push to the teacher. Once finished, the teacher is notified that they will show the screen, and from there, teachers can essentially do the same thing by showing students their screen. You don't need to have to show a screen anymore, since it's all there.

Here is how the various members of the Classroom can install the extension:

G Suite for Education accounts Administrator-the administrators are allowed to pre-install the extension for their organization members. This will reduce troubleshooting problems, save time, and ensure that teachers and students start straight away by using the extension.

Teachers-if you are a teacher in the classroom, you are allowed to install the extension.

Students-teachers can give the installation instructions to the students, and they will be able to install it.

Administrators

Only the G Suite for Education account members is allowed to pre-install the extension for their organization members. The installation can be done by following the steps given below:

Begin by signing into your Google Admin Console. Ensure that you sign in using your administrator account.

Click "Device management" from the dashboard.

Click "Chrome management" then "User settings".

Choose the organizational unit that you need to configure the settings for. If you need configuring the settings for all individuals in the organizational unit, choose the top-level unit. Or you can choose any of the child organizational units.

Click "Manage force-installed apps" at "Apps and Extensions," and closer to "Force installed Apps and Extensions".

Click the "Chrome Web Store" then search for "Share to Classroom".

Click Add then Save next to the extension.

The extension will then be installed successfully.

Teachers

Teachers are also allowed to install the Share to Classroom extension. The installation can be done by following these steps:

First, open the following URL:

https://chrome.google.com/webstore/detail/shareto-classroom/adokjfanaflbkibffcbhihgihpgijcei

Click the "Add to Chrome" button.

A new window will pop up. Click "Add extension".

The Share to Classroom icon will be shown to the right of chrome's address bar.

Click the icon to open the Share to Classroom extension.

Note that you must be signed into chrome to be able to use the Classroom.

You will have installed the extension successfully as a teacher.

As the teacher, you should post the Share to Chrome installation instructions to the students. You can do this by following the steps given below:

Begin by opening the following link:

https://classroom.google.com/share?url=https%3A%2F%2Fg.co%2Fsharetoclassroom&body=Open%20the%20following%20link%20to%20install%20the%20Share%20to%20Classroom%20Chrome%20extension&title=Install%20the%20Share%20to%20Classroom%20Chrome%20extension

Just copy and paste it in your Chrome browser. It will take you to the following page:

Click "Choose class," then select a class.

You should now choose the post type. Just click "Choose an action".

Choose any of the following:

Create an assignment

Ask question

Make an announcement

Click the Go button.

You can then select any of the following to post the instructions:

for the case of an assignment, click Assign.

For the case of a question, click Ask.

For the case of an announcement, click Post.

You can then click View to see how it appears on the class Stream.

Students

If you are a student, you can install the Share to Classroom extension if the teacher has posted the installation instructions on the classroom. Just follow the steps given below:

First, log into your Google Classroom account.

Identify and click the class.

On your post, click "Share to Classroom - Chrome Web Store."

Click the "Add to Chrome" option.

Click "Add extension".

You will be able to see the Share to Classroom icon to the right side of Chrome's address bar. Open the extension by clicking the Share to Classroom icon. Note that you must be signed into Chrome to be able to use the extension.

Tips when using Share to Classroom

The following tips will help you when you are using the Share to Classroom extension:

The extension will interrupt students once you "push" a link, so ensure that you "push" during the right times. Students are only allowed to share with the teacher, not the whole class. Teachers will have to model the appropriate use. Nothing can replace good classroom management.

G Suite Training

This is a free training on-demand for students and teachers, and it includes in time training on the Google Classroom. On the part of teachers, it means that you can get help and have your questions answered on the go while working inside the Google Classroom.

To see the G Suite Training sessions, follow the steps given below:

Use your G Suite credentials to sign in to Chrome.

Navigate to the G Suite service that you need to learn.

Click on the Training menu, that is, Training for G Suite Menu, to get a list of relevant lessons. You are also provided with a search feature that you can use to search for the lessons that you need.

Choose the lesson then the on-screen instructions to accomplish what you need.

Students are also allowed to use this extension to get help on how to navigate through the Google Classroom. It is a great way of orienting students at the start of a class or a semester to make sure that they will have a smooth experience using Google Classroom.

Configuring Portal Permissions

The super administrators for G Suite can determine the users who see Users, Reports, and Lessons pages in G Suite Training Portal. By default, users who have been assigned administrator roles are allowed to access all the pages. In contrast, users who are not assigned administrator roles are only allowed to see the Videos, Lessons, and Support pages.

The following steps will help you to configure the portal permissions:

Log into the G Suite Training Portal then click Users.

Click "Import from Google". The portal will import the user and organizational unit data. You are allowed to choose the organizations that you need to import.

Choose one or more users.

In the section for Manage Admin Permissions, choose the permissions that you need to add or remove.

Click either "Remove from selected" or "Add to selected".

You are allowed to generate usage reports from the portal. You only have to click Reports and see how the domain uses the G Suite Training. The page contains charts showing the number of lessons that have been completed by top users in the domain. Note the courts will only be shown once your organization has begun to use the lessons. The page will also allow you to generate reports having other data, like the specific lessons that each user has completed and the amount of time taken to complete the lesson.

To see training data for all the users, click "Generate New Report". If you need to specify or set the scope for the report, click "Show

Advanced Options" then "Generate New Report".

The generation of the report may take a minute, so remain patient. Once the report becomes ready, you can find it beneath the charts on the Reports page. You can download it by clicking Ready next to a report. Note that the report comes in a CSV format.

Add Materials

The best thing about Google Classroom is you can attach to these various videos, surveys, PDFs, and other items that you can utilize from Google drive. Students can, with this draw on, write down notes, and even highlight various elements with the PDFs within the classroom app to make it easier.

Customize the Class Color

Class themes and colors are something that you can integrate into the classroom. You can, with this, go to the settings, and then choose the default color or a theme for your class. This does help if you are working with multiple classes and want to make sure you provide the information to the correct class.

Assignment calendar

The assignment calendar has the purpose of keeping both students and teachers better organized. Each time a teacher creates something within Google Classroom, with a date on it, you will have it immediately on the class calendar. It is easily found by going to the three lines on the left corner area of your screen, and from there choosing calendar. Once displayed, you can see all of the work that has been assigned, whether you are a teacher assigning work to a class, or a student getting work from the teacher.

New Work Area

The new work area within Google Classroom does have assignments that are outstanding within one place. If a teacher does not grade an assignment yet, it will be there, which is suitable for students who are curious about whether or not something was graded. In the same vein, if a student has not turned in something yet, it will also show up there, so it is good for teachers to find out what they need to grade and useful for students who need to figure out what it is that they need to finish up.

Communication with others

Communication with parents and students alike is something that Google Classroom does decently, despite the lack of a live feature. The students can put posts to the stream of the classroom, which in many cases can be a good discussion board, and it is good if you do not want to have the question answered right away, or it is to a dire need. Many times, if you need to contact the teacher directly, there is a means to email them, and teachers can do the same. The stream is moderated by teachers as well, and you can attach media to each of these. Gmail also allows students and teachers to communicate on the interface. Moreover, with the introduction of the classroom apps, it allows for more integration there as well.

Archive courses

You can also archive courses with this. With Google Classroom, at the end of a semester or year, you can choose the course, go to settings, and from there, and archive it. It is removed from the main homepage, but it is not permanently deleted, so teachers can look at the current year and look for any assignments they want to keep. You can view it, but you cannot make changes. Deleting a class completely gets rid of it in its entirety, and many teachers decide not to do that, especially if they have assignments they enjoyed from the previous semester.

Organizing Stream

You can utilize topics to better organize streams. Every time an announcement is created, teachers can assign the topic to the category for every post, and let it be organized. Whenever it is created, the topic will be on the left-hand side of the stream, and when it is selected, the topic will show up. This allows teachers to put together content within the course, so you can organize the class into different units. This is great for history or biology teachers, who tend to need different units for everything they go over.

One-Click Worksheets

With every worksheet, you can create individual documents for every single one of them with a single click. This a nice feature that saves you time, so you don't need to copy everything to every single student since that can get quite annoying.

Class Resource Page

One remarkable feature of Google Classroom is the fact that you can always create a class resource page for any documents that you need to utilize with your class, including the rules and the syllabus. To do this is first to go to the classwork page, and from there, you choose settings and then choose to add class materials with a title on there, which will help organize the class a little bit better. You can always add multiple different resources under a singular title, and then add them with different names each time. You can then choose to attach and then choose the relevant icon. You can, from there, choose the item you want to add and then add either upload or add. To put a link on there, you can always click on that or add a link, and you can always press X to remove the attachment, and then press the option to post. If you have it in each section, it allows students to go to it at any time, which is ideal if they need to review the syllabus once again.

Exporting Grades

You can always export the grades you have to Google sheets or to a CSV file to see all the grades at once. You can only do it on the computer version, so you can't work on mobile. To do this, you click on your class, go to classwork, the assignment, and then choose to view it. You want to go to student work and then press the gear icon, and from there, you will want to copy all the grades to Google sheets, and then, you will be able to see the spreadsheet in the drive folders.

If you want to export the grades to a CSV file, you essentially do the same thing. You can choose whether you want to download the specific grades as CSV, or if you want to download all of the assignment grades as a CSV, and they'll be in the downloads folder so you can externally import this.

Creating Individual Assignments

Google Classroom also allows teachers to create individual assignments. In turn, this allows students to have a personal assignment if they need it, which is good if there is a chance that they need to do something specific, and this also can be used for announcements as well. It is quite nice, and you will realize when you use this that it is easy to implement, and simple to organize your assignments with.

Google classroom Apps

Activity Learn

This is an app that works super well with Google Classroom. It is good not just for languages, but also for English, social studies, and even biology. This one works well with Google Classroom, and you can even jigsaw, take the entire class, and even closely read some of the different aspects. Teachers can use this app if they want to bring some great and integrative activities in the classroom. Moreover, all of the assignments do synchronize back to Google Classroom.

Aladdin

This is more of an app for teachers than it is for students themselves, but Google Classroom fully integrates with Aladdin. That way, teachers can plan the roll, create grades, and also put together reports too. Teachers can also find information in a super quick manner, meaning that they can find out the date the student enrolled, their parent, the class, or the staff information, along with any relevant documents in a singular lace. The rulebook also will even be integrated with other apps that allow for alerts to be given in an absence, especially if they're in other classes, any trends of students, and also, to help reward the attendance of a student so that they feel better. It allows for a more integrative system of learning for students and teachers alike.

Uncheck

This is a great option for Google Classroom in that it offers a great paper similarity scanning resource for students and teachers, to eliminate plagiarism in the classroom. If you are a teacher who does have assignments that involve research, use this to check the assignments to make sure everything is original and not stolen from anywhere. If you are a student, it is good to use this since it will prove your authorship in the future if there is any potential issue, and you need to defend it. So what makes it different from another plagiarism checking? Well, it has different functions specifically for educators, in that the checker will recognize any reference sand citations, which are common in most papers that are written. It allows for it to work in real-time to check various databases, and it is one of the best for integration into Google Classroom.

Duolingo

For language students and teachers, this is the app for you. It can be hard to learn languages, and for teachers, it can also be quite frustrating, but Duolingo is one of the best apps out there, and it involves a lot of activities to help those learning languages. It's got 23 language options to offer, from Spanish to French to even Japanese, so you can learn the language by using this app. The lessons are small, and you can even record yourself talking to see what it sounds like, and to help with pronunciations. It is quite nice, and it will even let you have conversations with bots. It's one of the best apps for those who are looking to learn languages, and it's free to download.

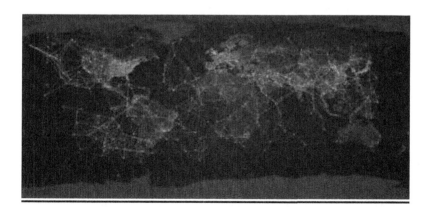

Quizzes

This isn't just any old quiz making app for teachers to use. Still, it actually makes the quizzes easy to understand, are educational games, and it allows you to assign homework and content related to it. It is in the form of a quiz game that makes it fun for students and teachers and the like.

What teachers do is they create a quiz using one of the pre-made ones, and then they assign it.

While they play, the teachers control the timer and leaderboard, allowing for it to show any knowledge gaps that need to be honed, and anything worth working on for everyone. It's a great quiz system that is perfect for review time with students if needed.

GoGuardian

This is a great tool not just for teachers, but administrators, and even counselors too.

You can filter the settings for students, get less few false positives, and even allow for better classroom management with the assisted tools, and with geolocation enabled on this, it allows for any devices that are lost or stolen the chance to recover.

This is great for using laptops in school as well. For teachers, it also allows students to show you what they are doing in real-time, create an activity timeline, and some scenes, which essentially allows for better working places, and less distraction.

With GoGuardian, you can integrate this with Google Classroom to ensure that students are creating a better environment for themselves, and teachers are less distracted as a result too.

Little Sis for Classroom

You can use this to create rosters that are integrative, and allow teachers to archive the classes not needed, and allow for the better and more efficient organization for teachers, and to make it more efficient for teachers as well.

There is a classroom explorer, which allows one to have insight on the classroom adoption, and allows for administrative actions on the classes too. With the sync jobs function, it will maintain everything in one place. It also has a more centralized guardian system, so in places where you need to have everything all put together, you can look at the current state of the guardian invites, and from there, send guardian invites to students. It is run manually initially, but it actually goes full automaton once it is started, and it is really nice if you run lots of classes, and need a good app for that.

Alma

This is another student information system, but it is the first to do the job of fully integrating with Google Classroom.

Throughout the integration, teachers can utilize this to synchronize the grades and assignments, and it can also be used with teaching teams to manage everything across the districts and the schools that are in the vicinity, which allows for better organization.

It's nice because it will showcase the different trends, and allow one to see what is happening, which is great if you're looking to ensure that you've kept up with everything in the school.

CK-12

This is a very handy app for students that features over 5000 different spelling, science, and math concepts along with lessons, and students can access this content wherever they are.

If your students need some extra resources to learn a subject, this is one of the best ways to do it.

Students can learn at the pace that is comfy with them, track their own personal progress on the subjects, and from there, even work on assignments and get deadline notices, and even recommendation for learning resources they can utilize, and a lot more.

It covers everything from basic concepts to even geometry and biology and calculus, and it is a major resource that will work for different educational levels.

Curiosity by Beacon Solutions

This is an app that allows students to have all the knowledge that they want easily, and it's one of the best apps for Google Classroom. Curiosity is one that is perfect for those students who do not want to stop learning, and you can learn a ton through using this. There are 5000 different articles and a million different videos on any topic imaginable, so you can use this with practically every grade level out there, and no matter the subject.

Whether you're using this to understand science, or better utilize this for history and other subjects, the videos and the articles that are there will tell others about the subjects, and in turn create items in a rewarding and beneficial manner.

Discovery Education

This is an app that gives digital media, textbooks, curricular resources, and videos for so many different subjects. Most of the major disciplines, including math and science, are available here. It is a great streaming resource too, and it even contains modules, personalized instructions, and guidelines that will help. It's more than just a streaming source, though, but it also has interactive features that help with assignments, including skill builders, audio clips, and even activities and assessments. It allows expending in the classroom more from a more static to engaging sorts of experiences for yourself.

Padlet

Students can also collaborate on the app, and they can work to put a lot of this together. It is one of the coolest and most rewarding apps currently in the classroom, so many teachers like this for partner projects, not just for art students. This is also good for if you want students to collaborate and work together on simple assignments, in that it's got videos, interviews, the ability to upload documents, and even writing out texts and theme customization. You can create discussion boards, Venn diagrams, or even business plans for business students. This is an app that allows you to do so much, and it is a fun one for students and teachers alike!

With some of these integrations, you will be able to utilize the apps that are easy and create an interactive learning environment that you and others will enjoy. Google Classroom has so much to offer, and so many different elements that teachers and students alike will enjoy this, since it offers a lot for them to utilize, and different aspects of this as well.

Additional Features in the Google Classroom

Rubrics

Teachers can create and reuse the rubrics. After the students have completed their work, they can check the assignments' rubric to monitor and track their work. When teachers grade rubrics, level selections automatically determine a total grade that can be adjusted manually also. After the assignment is returned, students can access their rubric feedback.

Moreover, rubrics are:

Customizable – Can add up to 50 criteria and 10 performance levels.

Shareable – Import/export options when you create an assignment.

Reusable – Reuse a rubric in multiple assignments.

Share to Classroom

This is an extension made for teachers who want to share web pages to the entire classroom, instantly happening on all student's computers. This is good if you're teaching a lesson, and you want to show it to every student because they won't have to sift through to try to find the web page, and it'll keep them on the right track. It is also used for announcements, assignments, and various web pages you want to share.

Power Thesaurus

For many students, power thesaurus is a way for students to look up various antonyms or synonyms for anything that they desire. When you have this on, you can double click the word from the icon on the toolbar, and then show off what that or any similar or dissimilar words mean. This is perfect if a student or even a teacher wants to beef up their own personal vocabulary.

Save to Google Drive

This is a great way for students doing research projects to save all of their content to Google drive. This saves so much time, especially if you're already working on the other Google tools as well. By enabling this, you can save anything you want, whether it be screenshots, pictures, or even web content, and throw it directly onto the drive itself, to make your life all the easier. It can change your productivity, and pairing it with the other tools can miraculously change it, too.

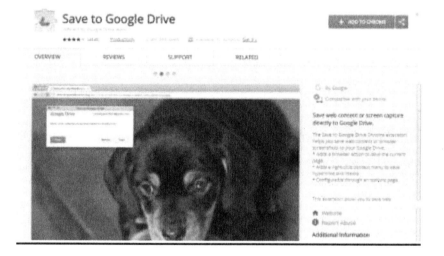

LastPass

One thing that can be frustrating and annoying for both students and teachers, especially if there is educational software that they use, is the number of passwords they have to remember. With LastPass, you'll be able to manage all your passwords and have them saved. Of course, this does have a couple of privacy concerns, but it works if you're just sick of trying to remember a million different passwords and want it all managed in a simplified manner.

Google URL Shortener

This is good for teachers who want to share many websites. If you're talking to students and want to link something to them, it can be a bit distracting. This is also a bit annoying if you're a teacher who likes to add links, but they're lines long. With the goo.gl URL shortener, you'll be able to shorten any URL by just clicking it. You can also make some QR codes to send to other students and teachers, and if you're using handouts and want to share the URL, you can do so easily. It's quite a time-saver and makes your life simpler.

G Suite Training

This is a free extension that works wonders for teachers and students, and if you have any question on whether to use this software, it is ultimately the way to go. You can get tutorial videos, interactive training, and even customer support help if you need it. What's more, if you're a student who has issues, don't think this is limited to just teachers, because students can also learn through these videos how to navigate through the Google Classroom software, and from there, be able to accomplish all the tasks that they have on hand. It's quite simple.

Read&Write

This is a great extension if you're casting your screen, and you want to read it out loud. This is also good for students who want to multitask various articles and hear what's being read. This is a great extension that essentially reads out loud what is on there. This is good for those who are ESL or are dyslexic, since it allows them to better understand what they're reading, and it also can be used to help check grammar. It's like digital proofreading for students so that their content sounds good, or if you want to read something, but don't feel like staring at a screen, this is the extension that will help you.

Grammarly

If you're a student or a teacher, who wants to make sure they have their grammar and spelling correct, this is the way to do it. It's a great way to have a second set of eyes on everything, and this is a free chrome extension. Essentially, it revises anything that's typed in and gives you correction suggestions to make it easier. While it may not always be correct, it allows you to have explanations that offer good options to try. It's a great extension to help with student and teacher learning.

Adblock

Ads are annoying. AdBlock is one of those extensions that you should always have. You can get just general AdBlock, but it is also AdBlock for YouTube, which allows you to literally block all the ads that come from YouTube, so you can browse without being distracted. Have you ever wanted to showcase a video, only to find out that it's got ads all over the place that are utterly annoying? Well, you can eliminate that with this extension, and just by downloading it, all of those annoying ads are gone.

Emoji for Chrome

This is a good one if you're going to send lots of messages to other students. Emojis are good to communicate sometimes, even just for an acknowledgment. It's easy if you want to have a way to find, use, and copy different emojis, and it's a good way to communicate with others on the web. After all, a good emoji might be just the right way to communicate with other people's various needs, or even how to respond to various assignments. Even a thumbs-up can be a good acknowledgment.

These extensions will change your ability to use Google Classroom, and for both students and teachers alike, it's a great way to really ensure you get the best results and to helps make your classroom experience better.

New Features with Gradebook

When it comes to grading, they have managed to make it a lot better and more streamlined for teaches to give them what they need. For starters, there is the grades page, which you can use now to record and return grades. There are actually new grading systems that you can select and put together, and from there, you can use that with each class. You also can look at the grade categories, and if you have different types of content, such as projects that are differently graded than quizzes, you can better organize this. You also can look at the way the grades are overall, and it definitely makes it easier too. There is now a Docs grading tool too, which you can use with your grades to help with assigning and changing this so that the grades for your documents are streamlined.

New Features

When you are choosing whether to archive a class, you can now do it on the mobile app for IOS. This means that when you're done, you do not need to just open up your phone each time, but instead, you can actively archive the class with no problems. You can also look at the student's page as well, and this is a new feature that has been added as well.

Finally, if you are looking to potentially try out the new beta programs, they are trying out the sync grades to your SIS program, which makes it easier for you to export your grades. For now, you can't' do it, but that is actually something that you can get from the beta. There is also the saving and using custom rubrics to grade the assignments and share that feedback to the students, too, again, another beta program that is worth trying out.

Drag and Drop classwork

This is another new feature of Google Classroom, and this actually helps to make it even more organized for teachers, so they can drag, and of course drop, the entire topic and items for classwork there, rearranging them easily on the page as well. You can drag the whole topic to one location on the classwork page itself, or bring it between the two, and it is a beta feature that is becoming more and more important with time. It is available on all platforms of the app currently.

New Themes

There is also the fact that there are now new themes that you can sue. This is great, especially for those teachers that want to keep all of their classrooms in order and if they teach multiple subjects. For example, history teachers can benefit from this, and you can now try new shapes, colors, iconography, and typography, all of which are available on both the web and the mobile app, making it easier to also add the class code too for students to join. There are now 78 themes currently, which range from history to hairdressing to photography, to math, which means that you can use this for more than the core academic subjects, you can use this for pretty much everything.

The Student Selector

This final feature's been added to the new Google Classroom that teachers are raving about. Student Selector allows for teachers to choose the student that they want, so if you're looking to put together groups or call people out to the class to answer questions, this is a new feature that you can use on iOS too, so if you have an iPhone, you can use this to your advantage. It can help to bring forth a new feature. There are ways to look at grading views too, and you will notice that this helps to bring forth a better, more integrative learning experience. With these new features, you can get the most that you can out of Google Classroom, and you will understand why people are loving this new system and understand as well why teachers are raving about using this in their learning environments these days.

Conclusion

This marks the end of this guide. Google Classroom is a good platform for the management of classes. It was developed by Google. It allows teachers to create an online classroom and invite students and co-teachers to join the classroom. The teacher can conduct most of the classwork online. This includes passing announcements to students, creating assignments, grading the assignments, and sending feedback to the students. Anytime you do an activity in the Classroom, the students are notified about the same via email. This makes it easy for the students to know when something new has been done and ensure that they are not left out by anything. It is more effective to track students' performance digitally compared to doing it manually. This is what Google Classroom does. It provides teachers and students with an online collaboration platform where they can collaborate with each other. The teachers and students can send messages to each other via email. With Google Classroom, teachers can digitally perform whatever that they usually need to perform manually.

Google Classroom is Google's online learning platform enabling teachers and students to do their daily lessons remotely in the classroom. Teachers can now monitor classes, build tasks, organize lesson notes and lesson plans with Google Classroom, and even score each student on-line.

If we could give something to teachers that would save them time, save the money from teaching, interact more with students and parents, support struggling with learners, and improve students' learning environment, will they consider using it? We hope they will.

Google Classroom streamlines the entire education cycle by removing the need for papers to be scanned and copied and entering grades manually into a grade book. Instead, it all happens online, saving time and energy. Teachers often save time and may focus on individual learning.

You can connect webpages from your mobile device to new tasks, questions, or updates in a class, without having to leave the page that you share. You can build a new assignment without going to the Classroom first if you see the Share to Classroom on a web page. Like the other social media icons on the website, you can consider Link to Classroom.

Setting up an account with Google Classroom is free and easy. Set up an account and navigate your way through the various windows to get a feel for how it flows. Even if you're not extremely technically literate, you'll find it to be an intuitively designed program.

The transition to a digital classroom doesn't have to be all or nothing. You can integrate the aspects of the virtual interface that seem to suit your needs, gradually introducing more technology into your classroom, without sacrificing the in-person atmosphere you've crafted over the years.

Always remember that your Google Classroom interface should be an active, living environment. It will be the most successful when students use it as a resource for collaboration and higher learning, rather than simply a place to take a few quizzes and turn in assignments.

Just like your classroom, the more feedback Google receives about the interface, the better they're able to adjust it to suit the needs of real-life teachers. If you ever notice any features that you think are missing or aren't being utilized to their full potential, send feedback suggesting a change. Google often updates the interface based on user feedback.

The more tools are available to teachers that help them better manage their time and resources, the more energy they're able to devote to actually teaching. If you are a teacher in any capacity, the variety of time-saving tools available on Google Classroom are, at the very least, worthy of investigation.

Since the information utilization is productive, it tends to be utilized from anyplace. That can mean a home web association, a Wi-Fi association, or even use over telephone information organize. Getting disconnected is likewise conceivable, it permits students to work from anyplace, realizing their endeavors will be transferred when their gadget interfaces with a system once more.

Printed in Great Britain
by Amazon